€ 4.⁰⁰

W9-AKT-526

THE

The Opera House Album

A COLLECTION OF TURN-OF-THE-CENTURY POSTCARDS

DESCRIBED BY

Charles Osborne

A CRESCENDO BOOK

TAPLINGER PUBLISHING COMPANY

New York

For Kenneth Thomson who loves
opera houses too

First published in the United States in 1979 by
TAPLINGER PUBLISHING CO., INC.,
New York, New York.

Copyright © by Charles Osborne.
All rights reserved.
Printed in Hungary.

Library of Congress Catalog Card Number: 79-64978
ISBN 0 8008 5836 0

No part of this book may be reproduced or transmitted in any form or by any means, electronic or mechanical, including photocopy, recording, or any information storage and retrieval system now known or to be invented, without permission in writing from the publisher, except by a reviewer who wishes to quote brief passages in connection with a review written for inclusion in a magazine, newspaper or broadcast.

Browsing in a second-hand book shop in Vienna a year or two ago, I came across a photograph album which contained a collection, neatly mounted, of turn-of-the-century postcards of old theatres and opera houses. Many of them were theatres in small towns, outposts of the old Austro-Hungarian Empire. Some of the towns have changed their names and their countries as a result of the central European wars of this century; several of the theatres disappeared during the 1939–45 war. The collection had originally belonged to a Viennese musician who had apparently instructed his family, friends, pupils and colleagues to send him post-cards of theatres and opera houses in the towns they visited on travels abroad, for the majority of the cards are addressed to him: for example, the card from Brünn (now Brno, in Czechoslovakia) from one Otto Czech is addressed on the verso to 'Wohlgeboren Herrn Emil Wipperich, Professor am Conservatorium, Wien I, Giselastrasse 12.'

From the archives of the Vienna State Opera, which in Professor Wipperich's time was the K. u. K. Hofoper (Imperial and Royal Court Opera), I have discovered that Emil Wipperich was also a horn player in the Vienna Philharmonic Orchestra, which provided and still provides the orchestra for the Opera. The period of his engage-ment was from 1 April 1882 to 31 March 1914. Most of the cards were posted to him between 1897 and 1908, though two of them, those of Hellbrunn and Marienbad, date from 1914. The cards of Viennese theatres which were included in the album were the only ones not to have been sent through the post. They contain no message on the verso: the majority of the others contain greetings, messages from colleagues fulfilling an engagement at one or other of these theatres, or family gossip. Several are from Alfred Holy, a harpist in the orchestra from 1903 to 1913. One, from another horn player Professor Hermann Moissl, who joined the orchestra on 1 January 1899 and was still a member in 1945, is addressed to Wipperich at the Bayreuth Festspiel. Evidently Professor Wipperich played in the Bayreuth orchestra during his summer holidays. 'Die Kur hat mir gut getan' ('The cure has done me good) writes his sister Anna from the spa at Marienbad.

I have chosen a selection from the album, concentrating on the lesser-known theatres, many of which no longer exist. The cards are attractive and evocative objects, mementoes of a lost world, and inducers of an innocent and pleasurable *Sehnsucht.*

CHARLES OSBORNE

3

AACHEN, *Germany (B.R.D.)*
STADTTHEATER

DESIGNED by Baurat (i.e. Government Surveyor) Johann Peter Cremer with Karl Friedrich Schinkel as advisor, the theatre took three years to build, and was opened in 1825. Like most German and Austrian civic theatres, other than those in capital cities, it was used for opera and operetta as well as drama. The theatre was partly rebuilt and the stage reorganised by Heinrich Seeling in 1900–01. Many distinguished performers in opera and drama began their careers here. Herbert von Karajan was chief conductor from 1934 to 1938, and Irmgard Seefried made her opera début at Aachen as the Priestess in *Aida* in 1939, remaining with the company until 1943. The theatre was destroyed towards the end of the Second World War. It was rebuilt and opened again in 1951.

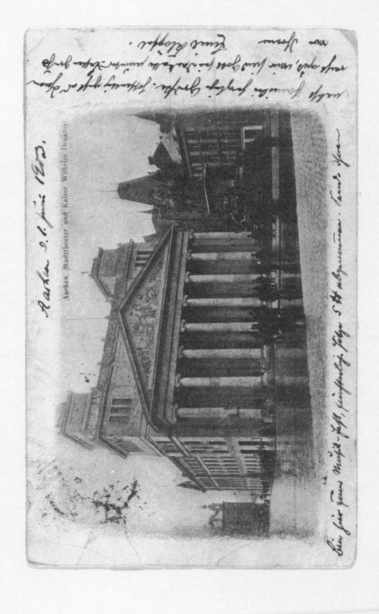

Aachen, Stadttheater und Kaiser Wilhelm Denkmal.

ALTENBURG, *Germany* (*D.D.R.*)
HOFTHEATER

OPENED on 11 January 1843 with Lortzing's *Zar und Zimmermann*, the theatre shown here was a later and almost identical copy of Gottfried Semper's more famous Dresden Hoftheater (1838–41) and was built between 1869 and 1871. Projected by the local Baurat Enger, the work was carried out by Otto Brückwald (the architect who executed Wagner's conception of the Bayreuth Festspielhaus, 1872–76). An additional foyer, grander staircases and a new façade were built in 1904. The theatre, renamed the Landestheater in 1919, is still in use for opera and drama, and seats almost 1100. The square it faces is now called the Rosa-Luxemburg Platz.

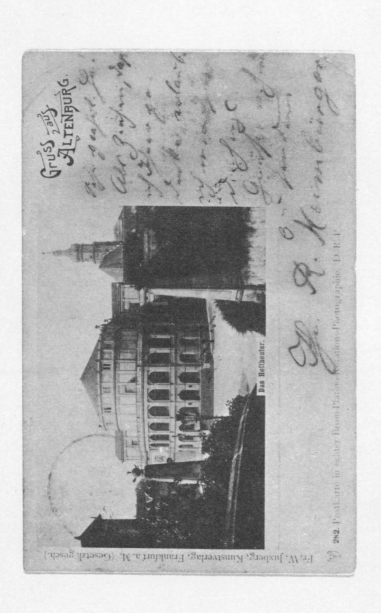

7

ALTONA, *Germany* (*B.R.D.*)
STADTTHEATER

ESIGNED by the Hamburg architects, Hansen and Meerwein, and seating 1000, the principal theatre of Altona, the dock area of Hamburg, was built in 1875–76 and opened on 20 September 1876 with a performance of Goethe's *Egmont*, the incidental music being by Beethoven. Run on co-operative lines, it produced opera as well as plays.

Altona

Stadttheater

Dr. Trenkler Co., Leipzig. 4138

9

BAYREUTH, *Germany* (*B.R.D.*)

OPERNHAUS

BAYREUTH's Markgräfliches Opernhaus was built in 1745–48 by Joseph Saint-Pierre with decorations by Giuseppe and Carlo Galli-Bibiena done between March and September 1748. It was designed for the Margrave Friedrich of Bayreuth and his wife the Margravine Wilhelmine, who was a sister of Frederick the Great. The Margravine had Von Knobelsdorff's plans for the Berlin Staatsoper sent to her in 1743, and then chose Saint-Pierre as her architect. The theatre opened on 23 September 1748 with Hasse's *Ezio*. Still completely intact, the Opernhaus is the most elaborate Baroque-Rococo theatre extant. It was completely restored in 1935–36.

Gruss aus Bayreuth

Opernhaus

1281 F. H. A. 1902 Nachdruck verboten

11

BAYREUTH, *Germany* (B.R.D.)
RICHARD WAGNER THEATER

THE Richard Wagner Festspielhaus is, without doubt, the most famous and prestigious of German opera houses. In 1871 Wagner persuaded the citizens of this small Bavarian town to provide him with the land, on a hill just outside the town, on which a theatre could be constructed which would exist to stage his own music dramas. The foundation-stone of the building was laid at a ceremony in 1872 and the theatre opened in 1876 with the first complete performance of Wagner's *Ring* tetralogy: *Das Rheingold* (13 August), *Die Walküre* (14 August), *Siegfried* (16 August) and *Götterdämmerung* (17 August). Originally intended only as a temporary structure, the brick and wooden auditorium, seating 1800, still stands, and a summer festival of Wagner performances continues to be held annually. After 1944 when all the German

theatres closed, Bayreuth did not reopen until 1951. Winifred Wagner, the composer's daughter-in-law who had directed the festivals from 1931 to 1944, was forced to retire from the enterprise because of her friendship with Hitler, and post-war Bayreuth was managed for several years by her sons Wieland and Wolfgang. Since Wieland's death the festival has been under the sole direction of Wolfgang Wagner.

The basic revolutionary conception of the Festspielhaus with its steeply-raked single bank of seats, fan-shaped in a simple auditorium, was Wagner's own. He had first tried out his ideas with his close friend Gottfried Semper, the architect of the Dresden Hoftheater, in the abortive scheme for a Festspielhaus in Munich in 1865. For Bayreuth he used Otto Brückwald as executant architect.

BAYREUTH. Richard-Wagner-Theater.

VERLAG (BAYREUTHER WAGNER MUSEUM) COPE GRAHEL

BAYREUTHER KUNSTBLATT N°1

13

EAST BERLIN, Germany (D.D.R.)
KÖNIGLICHES OPERNHAUS

THE former Royal Opera House of Prussia is now the Staatsoper or State Opera of the East German capital. Built in the reign of Frederick the Great to designs by Baron Georg Wenzeslaus von Knobelsdorff, the theatre in Berlin's spacious boulevard Unter den Linden was opened in 1742 with a performance of Graun's opera, *Cleopatra e Cesare*. Graun was the theatre's manager and chief composer for fifteen years, during which time he produced twenty-six of his own operas.

Among important premieres during the nineteenth century were Weber's *Der Freischütz* (1821), Nicolai's *Die Lustigen Weiber von Windsor* (1849), and Meyerbeer's *Das Feldlager in Schlesien* (1844) which was written for Jenny Lind. For a time, Meyerbeer was Music Director, and Nicolai one of the two chief conductors under his administration. When a fire virtually destroyed the opera house in 1843, it was immediately rebuilt, almost to the same plans, by Carl Ferdinand Langhans. In the late nineteenth and early twentieth centuries, though very few new works of importance were first produced in the theatre, the level of performance reached new heights under such conductors as Felix Weingartner and Richard Strauss. After the First World War and the collapse of the German

monarchy, the now re-named Staatsoper became one of Europe's leading opera houses. Its principal conductors included Leo Blech, Erich Kleiber, Otto Klemperer, Wilhelm Furtwängler and Clemens Krauss, though only Furtwängler and Krauss continued into the Nazi period. Important new works first produced at the Staatsoper during this time included Alban Berg's *Wozzeck* (1925), Darius Milhaud's *Christophe Colomb* (1930) and Hans Pfitzner's *Das Herz* (1931).

The Staatsoper's company during the thirties and forties contained virtually all of Germany's finest singers: Frida Leider, Tiana Lemnitz, Erna Berger, Margarete Klose, Maria Müller, Gerhard Hüsch, Heinrich Schlusnus, Helge Roswaenge, Franz Völker and Marcel Wittrisch. When the theatre was destoyed by bombs in 1945, the company transferred to the Admiralspalast, a former operetta theatre. The Staatsoper opened, having again been rebuilt to Von Knobelsdorff's original designs, in 1955 in a now-divided Berlin. It is one of East Berlin's two leading opera houses, performing a fairly conventional repertory and leaving more controversial works and productions to the Komische Oper of Walter Felsenstein and his successor Joachim Herz.

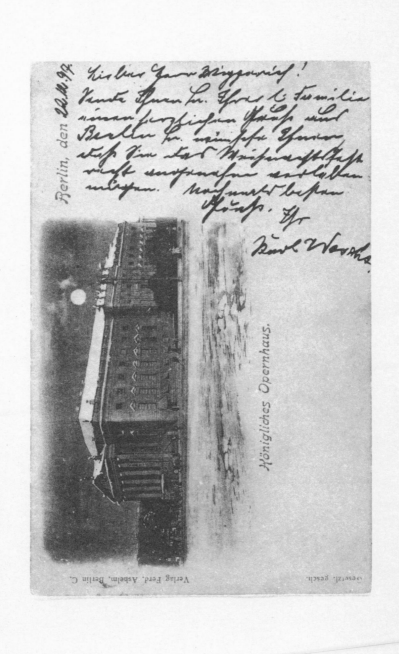

WEST BERLIN, *Germany* (*B.R.D.*)
LESSING THEATER

ESIGNED by J. Hennicke and H. von der Hude, the Lessing Theater was built in 1887–88 and opened on 11 September 1888 with Lessing's *Nathan der Weise*. It cost £40,000 to build, and seated 1170. Although the theatre was conceived as a house for contemporary dramatists, its first director Dr Oskar Blumenthal, a well-known Berlin critic, chose to open with Lessing. He failed to make the theatre successful along the lines originally laid down, and left in 1898. The theatre no longer exists, having been destroyed during the last war.

Lessing-Theater.

Gruss aus Berlin.

511 L. Saalfeld, Berlin S.W. 29.

17

WEST BERLIN, *Germany* (*B.R.D.*)
KROLL'SCHES ÉTABLISSEMENT

THE importance of Kroll's theatre in European operatic history is confined to the years 1927–31 when it functioned as an opera house under the direction of Otto Klemperer. The theatre had been acquired by the state as early as 1896, the intention being to pull it down and build a new opera house on the site. Various difficulties delayed these plans, and eventually the dilapidated theatre was repaired and partly rebuilt. Now named the Oper am Königsplatz, it opened in 1924 with Wagner's *Die Meistersinger* conducted by Erich Kleiber. When the square in which it was situated was renamed in 1926, the theatre became the Oper am Platz der Republik, though it continued to be known to habitués as the Kroll-oper. Under Klemperer, the Kroll company became the leading avant garde opera organisation in Europe, producing such new works as Kurt Weill's *Royal Palace* (1927) and Paul Hindemith's *Neues vom Tage* (1929) and staging new and original productions of popular repertory pieces including *Madama Butterfly*, *Der fliegende Holländer* and *Die Fledermaus*.

The worsening political situation closed the Kroll in 1931, and Klemperer conducted unwillingly and unhappily at the Staatsoper until 1933 when the Nazis cancelled his contract. The theatre became the home of the German Reichstag when the Reichstag building was destroyed by fire. It did not survive the Second World War, and today no trace of it remains.

The building history of the Kroll is complicated. The Établissement Kroll, designed by Eduard Knoblauch, first opened on 15 February 1844 with a great ball. The place was a combination of three large halls, the largest being the Königssaal, as well as outdoor eating and entertainment facilities. Soon the Königssaal was given a stage at one end, and on 27 June 1850 a summer theatre was opened. The following year, on 1 February, the place burnt down, but was rebuilt by the architect Eduard Titz, and re-opened on 24 February 1852, the Königssaal having been transformed into a theatre seating 3000. The last and most thorough of the theatre's reconstructions was by the well-known theatre and cinema architect, Oskar Kaufmann (1873–1942) in 1922–23.

Kroll'sches Etablissement

E. B. W. 3612.

Berlin 22/6 02

19

WEST BERLIN, *Germany* (*B.R.D.*)
SCHILLER THEATER

The theatre shown on the postcard was built in 1863–64 by the architect Eduard Titz, and seated approximately 1230. It was rebuilt around 1900, and after Heilmann and Littman's Schiller Theater was opened in 1907 the older theatre had its name changed to Wallner Theater. The Wallners were an important Berlin theatre family whose descendants still work in the theatre in Germany. The first Wallner, Franz, was a mid-nineteenth-century actor-manager. The theatre does not now exist, having been destroyed, probably during the 1939–45 war. The 1907 Schiller Theater was bombed in the war but was later rebuilt, opening again in 1951. The present Schiller Theater houses West Germany's most important drama company, financed by the West Berlin Senate.

Berlin, 6. VII. 03.

Schiller-Theater.

Joh. Franke, Berlin S, No. 492.

WEST BERLIN, *Germany* (*B.R.D.*)

BERLINER THEATER

REBUILT in 1888 by the Architect G. Schnitger, the building was formerly the Walhalla Theater, an operetta and variety house designed by Oscar Titz. The Berliner was opened on 16 September 1888 by the actor-manager Ludwig Barnay, with Schiller's *Demetrius*. Barnay's company were early exponents of the Volkstheater movement: good plays for a popular audience. The Berliner, which no longer exists, seated 1200. It stood in Charlottenstrasse. The present Berliner Theater in Nürnbergerstrasse was opened in 1958.

WEST BERLIN, *Germany* (*B.R.D.*)
THEATER DES WESTENS

THE theatre, which seats 1642, was designed by Bernhard Sehring, built in 1895–96, and opened on 1 October 1896. Situated in Kantstrasse, in the Charlottenburg district of Berlin, it served for many years as a theatre for spoken drama as well as opera and operetta. From 1934 until the beginning of the Second World War it housed the Volksoper, whose Director and Chief Conductor was Erich Orthmann. The Volksoper policy was to stage the lighter operas and operettas.

At the end of the war, Berlin found itself divided into two cities, with the old Staatsoper (State Opera) now in the East, and the Deutsches Opernhaus, home of the Städtische Oper or Civic Opera, in the West. Both theatres had been destroyed in air-raids, and the West Berlin authorities moved the company of the Städtische Oper to the Theater des Westens in 1945. The bass-baritone Michael Bohnen became the theatre's Intendant, and the chief conductors included Robert Heger, Leopold Ludwig and Arthur Rother. In 1948 Heinz Tietjen was appointed to succeed Bohnen, and Leo

Blech and Ferencz Fricsay shared the musical direction. A new generation of German singers began to emerge, foremost among them the baritone Dietrich Fischer-Dieskau who made his début at the Theater des Westens as Rodrigo in Verdi's *Don Carlos* in 1948.

When the company of the Städtische Oper moved back into the rebuilt Deutsche Oper in the Bismarckstrasse in 1961, the Theater des Westens became the leading West Berlin theatre for musicals, musical comedies and operettas. A permanent company is maintained which, with the assistance of guest stars, performs a wide range of light musical works from *Die Fledermaus* to *Annie Get Your Gun.*

An inscription on the façade (noted by the writer, who attended a performance there of Benatzky's *Im weissen Rössl* in May 1976) reads: 'MDCCCXCVI BERNHARD SEHRING HANC DOMUM ARTIS COLENDAE CAUSA CONDIDIT'. (In 1896 Bernhard Sehring established this building for the encouragement of art.)

Gruss aus Charlottenburg, 1.9. 27. 01.

Theater des Westens.

Verlag Ernst Küssner, Berlin-Pankow. 101.

BERNBURG, *Germany* (*D.D.R.*)

THEATER

U NABLE to raise the money for construction, the citizens of this small Saxon town, which even now has only some 60,000 inhabitants, appealed to the Erbprinz Alexander-Karl von Anhalt-Bernburg. He commissioned the local Bauinspektor Johann August Philipp Bunge to design the theatre, which was constructed in 1826. It opened on 2 March 1827 with two plays by Friedrich Hoffmann, *Das Gelübde* and *Wolfgang von Anhalt*. Until 1881, when it was given to the town by the Duke of Anhalt-Dessau, the theatre was known as the Herzogliches Schauspielhaus.

After extensive restoration and modernisation by the Berlin architect, Eduard Titz, it opened as the Stadttheater on 4 January 1882 with Goethe's *Iphigenie*. Too small to support its own company, Bernburg saw touring productions, first from Dessau and later from Magdeburg. The theatre was again restored and re-equipped between 1926–28, opening this time with Mozart's *Marriage of Figaro* on 15 April 1928. The theatre is still in use, and its delightful early nineteenth-century atmosphere has been well preserved.

Bernburg,
Theater.

BERNDORF, *Austria*
KAISER FRANZ JOSEF THEATER

The theatre was built in 1898–99, its architects being Ferdinand Fellner and Herman Helmer, the famous Viennese partners who designed some eighty theatres, concert halls and casinos throughout Central Europe. It was opened on 27 September 1899 with a comedy, *Der kleine Mann* by Carl Karlwein. This tiny theatre, seating 488, was erected by Arthur Krupp of the Berndorfer Matallwarenfabrik as one of several amenities (hospitals, schools, baths etc.) for his workers. As its name implies it was also meant to commemorate the fiftieth anniversary of the Emperor Franz Josef's reign. The theatre, set in a park, is still in use. The municipality of Berndorf, a small industrial town of about 10,000 inhabitants in Lower Austria, seven miles south-west of Baden, restored the theatre in 1962–63.

Kaiser Franz Josef-Theater, Berndorf.

BIELSKO, *Poland*
STADTTHEATER

 BUILT in 1888–90 to designs by Emil Förstel, the theatre was subsequently modernized by Fellner and Helmer, and then seated 1000. It is used for both opera and drama. The town of Bielsko was formerly Bielitz, in Silesia, and part of the Austro-Hungarian Empire. It became part of Poland in 1919 but remained for many years predominantly a German-speaking town, and its theatre was thought of as essentially German-language.

Bielitz, 26. XII. 0 m. [handwritten]

Stadttheater.

31

BRAUNSCHWEIG, *Germany* (*B.R.D.*)
HERZOGLICHES HOFTHEATER

 IRST known as the Hoftheater, and then from 1919 as the Landestheater, since 1938 the theatre has been called the Braunschweig (or Brunswick) Staatstheater. Built between 1858 and 1861 by the architects Ahlberg and Wolf, it opened on 1 September 1861 with Goethe's *Iphigénie auf Tauris*. The first opera to be given was Wagner's *Tannhäuser*.

The interior and stage were rebuilt in 1902–04 by Heinrich Seeling. The theatre was damaged during the last war, but was restored, and re-opened with *Don Giovanni* on 28 December 1948. It is now used for large-scale productions of opera, drama and ballet, the seating capacity being 1247 as against a pre-war figure of 1600.

Gruss aus Braunschweig!

Herzogl. Hoftheater

BRNO, *Czechoslovakia*
STADTTHEATER

Brno, formerly Brünn, was a provincial Austro-Hungarian town when this theatre was built in 1881–82 by Fellner and Helmer. It opened on 30 October 1882 with Goethe's *Egmont* and is still in operation. It is now called Státní Divadlo (State Theatre) or Janáček Opera House.

The Moravian town of Brünn was the scene of the first performance of many of the operas of Leoš Janáček including *Jenůfa* (1904), *Katya Kabanova* (1921), *The Cunning Little Vixen* (1924), *The Makropoulos Affair* (1926) and *From the House of the Dead* (1930). Three of Martinů's operas also had their premieres there.

Stadttheater.

Heil!

Brünn. 10./190.

Erlaube mir Herrn Professor mitzutheilen, das ich seit 1. Sytem.
N. J. am Brünner Stadttheater als zweiter rother Heldtenor
engagiert bin und mich sehr wohlfühle. Hochachtend
Otto Ernst

BUDAPEST, *Hungary*

VIGSZINHÁZ (LUSTSPIEL THEATER)

OTH the Hungarian and German names of this theatre could be translated into English as Gaiety Theatre. Built in 1895–96 by Fellner and Helmer, it was opened on 1 May 1896 with a comedy, *A Barangók* by M. Jokai. Seating 1402, it continued to be used as a drama theatre until hit by a bomb in 1945. It was rebuilt in 1951 as an army theatre, the old exterior being retained but the interior completely redesigned. Since 1959 it has reverted to its former name, Vigszinház, and its former use. Emmerich Kalman's operetta, *Tatar-jaras* (produced in London in 1912 at the Royal Adelphi Theatre as *Autumn Manoeuvres*), had its world premiere at the Vigszinház in 1908.

Vigszinház. — Lustspiel-Theater. Budapest.

Törv. védve. — Ges. gesch. — 409. sz. Divald Károly Budapest

BUDAPEST, *Hungary*
KÖNIGLICHE OPER

THE former Hungarian Royal Opera is now the Magyar Állami Operaház, or State Opera House. Designed by Miklós Ybl, it now seats nearly 1400. The theatre's foundation stone was laid in September 1875 but financial difficulties prevented much work being done until 1882. It opened on 27 September 1884. It is famous as having the first hydraulic sinkable stage on the Asphaleia system in Europe. The entire building cost a mere £43,000. At the time of the postcard the auditorium seated 1250. The theatre is now the home of the national opera and ballet companies of Hungary. The opera company has had a number of distinguished chief conductors, among them Mahler, Nikisch and Klemperer, and the present company contains some excellent singers, several of whom are making international careers, among them the sopranos Eva Marton and Sylvia Sass.

Budapest. Királyi opera — Königliche Oper.

39

BYDGOSZCZ, *Poland*
STADTTHEATER

BYDGOSZCZ, formerly the German town of Brom-berg in the Polish Corridor, is an industrial town. Its Stadttheater was built in 1895–96 at a cost of £23,000 by Heinrich Seeling, and was considered to be one of his finest theatres. It was used for both opera and drama, but was destroyed in 1945 and has not been rebuilt.

CHEB, *Czechoslovakia*
STADTTHEATER

THE frontier town of Cheb in Western Czecho-slovakia, near Mariánské Lázně (Marienbad) and not far from Bayreuth, used formerly to be the Austro-Hungarian town of Eger. Its Stadttheater, 1873–74, now known in Czech as Městské Divadlo, was designed by Vincenc Pröckl, and built by Karel Haberzettl. It has undergone slight alterations and restoration at various times, but is still used for both opera and drama.

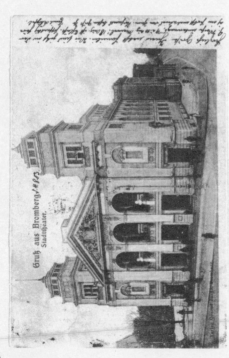

DARMSTADT, *Germany* (*B.R.D.*)
GROSSHERZOGLICHES THEATER

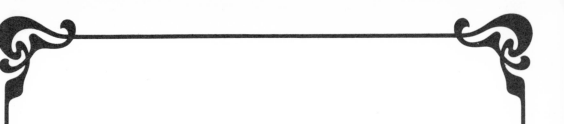

EATING 1370, the theatre was designed by Georg Moller and opened in 1819 with the opera *Fernand Cortez* by Spontini. In 1871 it was partly destroyed by fire, but was reopened in 1879, having been rebuilt (1875–79) to designs by Stadt-baumeister Christian Horst. It was reconstructed yet again, this time by Fellner and Helmer, in 1904–05 but was completely destroyed during the 1939–45 war.

Gruss aus Darmstadt

Grossherzogl. Theater.

DESSAU, *Germany* (*D.D.R.*)
HERZOGLICHES HOFTHEATER

ESIGNED by Carl Ferdinand Langhans, the Dessau Hoftheater was built in 1855–56 on the ruins of a more famous theatre by Friedrich Wilhelm von Erdmannsdorf which burnt down in 1855. (When it was constructed in 1798, Erdmannsdorf's theatre was the third largest in Germany, only Berlin and Bayreuth being able to boast larger theatres.) The Hoftheater as seen on the postcard was used principally for opera and ballet. Its stage was improved in 1883. The theatre was destroyed by fire in 1922, and was completely rebuilt by Lipp and Roth in 1935–38. During the war this new theatre was severely damaged, but was restored and reopened in 1949, the opening productions being Mozart's *Zauberflöte* and Brecht's *Mutter Courage*. The theatre became known as the Landestheater, Sachsen-Anhalt, in 1919, but is now simply called the Dessau Landestheater.

Gruss aus Dessau 11/9 i 99   Herzogl. Hoftheater

DRESDEN, *Germany* (*D.D.R.*)
KÖNIGLICHES HOFTHEATER

THE theatre depicted is the second Royal Opera House designed by Gottfried Semper. (The first, built to Semper's plans in the years 1837 to 1841, was opened in 1841. In 1842, Wagner's *Rienzi* had its premiere there, as did his *Fliegender Holländer* in 1843 and *Tannhäuser* in 1845. The theatre was destroyed by fire in 1869.) Built on the site of the first theatre, the second opened in 1878, having taken seven years to construct. At the turn of the nineteenth and twentieth centuries, the opera company in Dresden was considered to be one of the finest in Europe. A number of operas by Richard Strauss were given their first performances here, among them *Salome* (1905), *Elektra* (1909), *Der Rosenkavalier* (1911), *Intermezzo* with Lotte Leh-

mann (1924), *Arabella* (1933) and *Daphne* (1938). Busoni's *Doktor Faust* and Hindemith's *Cardillac* (both 1925) also had their premieres in Dresden. It was here that the German Verdi revival began in the late twenties. In February 1945 the theatre was almost completely destroyed during the air-raids. Since 1948, the opera company has performed in the former Schauspielhaus. The façade of the Semper Opera House has been preserved, the theatre is in the process of reconstruction, and is expected to reopen during 1977.

Gottfried Semper, who was assisted in the second building of the Hoftheater by his son Manfred, died in Rome in May 1879, soon after the theatre had opened.

Königl. Hoftheater mit König Johann-Denkmal.

14. Römmann Foy, Dresden.

Theaterprobe f. Dresd.'s ...
Dresden 25. August 1899.

Verehrter u. lieber Herr Collega! Sende Ihnen, meinem Versprechen gemäss, eine ...

FLENSBURG, *Germany* (*B.R.D.*)
STADTTHEATER

 LENSBURG in Schleswig-Holstein is Germany's most northerly town. Its city architect, Fielitz, built the theatre, which seats 601, in 1893–94. It opened on 23 September 1894 with a performance of Schiller's *Wilhelm Tell*. Opera, operetta, ballet and plays are still performed there by a resident company.

Gruss aus Flensburg. Stadttheater.

Platino-M. Reinicke & Rubin, Magdeburg.

FRANKFURT AM MAIN, *Germany* (*B.R.D.*)

OPERNHAUS

SEVERAL prominent citizens of Frankfurt con-
tributed funds in 1870 to build a house suitable
for grand opera. Work on the building was begun
in the spring of 1873 from designs by Lucas. When
he died in 1877, two of his assistants, Becker and
Giesenberg, completed the building which was
opened on 20 October 1880. At the time, it was
considered the best equipped opera house in the
world: it cost £230,000 to construct, more than four
times the amount its sponsors had stipulated.

The opera house was burnt out by a fire bomb
on 22 March 1944, only the shell of the building
remaining intact. For many years a scheme for
constructing a series of concert halls within this
shell has been under consideration. (In 1951,
Heinrich Seeling's Schauspielhaus, 1899–1902, was
remodelled as Frankfurt's opera house.)

Gruss

aus Frankfurt a. M. 10. 2. 99. Opernhaus.

Kunstverlag Garde & Loeb, Frankfurt a. M.

GENEVA, *Switzerland*
GRAND THEATRE

Built from 1875 to 1879 to designs by Jacques-Elisée Goss, who was much inspired by Garnier's Paris Opera (1861–74), the theatre was opened on 2 October 1879 with a performance of Rossini's *Guillaume Tell*. During a performance of *Die Walküre* in 1951 a fire broke out on stage and the theatre was almost totally destroyed, only the façade and foyer surviving. The stage and auditorium were rebuilt to designs by the architects Charles Schopfer of Geneva and Marcello Zavelani-Rossi of Milan, and the theatre, which now seats 1500, was reopened in 1962 with Verdi's *Don Carlos*. It is in use principally as an opera house, though it has housed performances of French drama by the Comédie-Française.

Genève - Le Théâtre

J.J. 649

53

GOERLITZ, *Germany (D.D.R.)*

STADTTHEATER

BUILT in 1850–51 by Eduard Titz, the theatre exists today in virtually its original form, despite various rebuilding operations. It is now known as the Gerhart-Hauptmann-Theater.

GRAZ, *Austria*

STADTTHEATER

THE theatre, designed by Peter von Nobile and built in 1824–25, opened in October 1825. It replaced an eighteenth-century theatre on the same site which had been destroyed by fire in 1823. First known as the Landisches Theater (Provincial Theatre), it became in 1887 the Stadttheater (Town Theatre). Partly demolished in 1959–60, it was rebuilt with an auditorium restored to its original form and opened again in 1964 as the Grazer Schauspielhaus or theatre for drama, seating 588. Opera is performed in the Opera House which opened in 1899.

Gruss aus Graz.
Stadttheater.

Stadttheater mit Demianplatz.

GOERLITZ, 12. I. 04.

Seimus, Professor! Ihr A. Holly

131. Lichtdruck von Robert Scholz, Görlitz.

HAMBURG, *Germany* (B.R.D.)
STADTTHEATER

THE first Stadttheater to appear on Dammtorstrasse was built in 1825–27 by Stadtbaudirektor Wimmel, after designs by Schinkel which had been somewhat modified. It opened on 3 May 1827, with Goethe's *Egmont*. The first opera performance was of Spohr's *Jessonda*, four days later. Until the building of the Thalia Theater in 1843, the Stadttheater was the principal opera and drama theatre of Hamburg. With the Thalia specializing in drama, the Stadttheater went over almost exclusively to opera, becoming known as the Grosse Oper in 1851. The house was rebuilt in 1873–74 by the Hamburg architect Martin Haller, when it acquired the aspect seen in the postcard. It was in this theatre that Gustav Mahler worked as music director from 1891 to 1897, and that Lotte Lehmann made her opera début in 1909.

The stage was completely rebuilt and greatly enlarged in 1925–26 by Diestel and Grubitz, the actual planning being done by the famous Professor Linnebach, a stage engineer who, between the wars, was responsible for much of the fantastically elaborate stage machinery for which the German theatre is noted. In 1933, the theatre became known as the Hamburg Staatsoper. It was bombed in 1943, and the auditorium burnt out. After the war, a provisional auditorium seating 606 was built on the stage which had suffered little damage. In 1949, this was enlarged into the burnt-out shell of the auditorium, and seated 1226. Some years later, the old auditorium was completely rebuilt, and new façades designed, by the Frankfurt architect Gerhard Weber. The theatre in its present form opened on 15 October 1955, and seats 1679.

Stadttheater

Stengel & Co. Dresden-Berlin. 8320

HANNOVER, *Germany* (*B.R.D.*)
KÖNIGLICHES THEATER

ow known simply as the Opernhaus, Hann-over's Königliches Hoftheater was built from 1845 to 1852 to designs by Georg Ludwig Laves, and opened on 1 September 1852 with Goethe's *Torquato Tasso*. The theatre was built for King Ernst August of Hannover, but was not finished until his son Georg V was on the throne. At that time the city had a population of no more than 28,000, whereas the theatre could seat as many as 2650. A contemporary source reveals that, in addition to grand balls, it was used for 'die Poesie, die Musik, die Tragödie, die ernste Oper, die komische Oper, das Schauspiel, das Lustspiel und der Tanz.'

In 1882, a rebuilding reduced the seating capacity to 1600. The theatre was burnt out in July 1943, the shell, however, remaining quite intact. A new interior was created by the architect Werner Kallmorgen, and the theatre reopened as Hann-over's opera house on 30 November 1950.

Königl. Theater.

Hannover.

HELLBRUNN, *Austria*
MECHANISCHES THEATER

The Mechanical Theatre or Felsentheater (Rock Theatre) at Schloss Hellbrunn, near Salzburg, dates from 1615, the year in which the baroque palace was built as the summer residence of Marcus Sitticus, Archbishop of Salzburg. The open-air theatre has 113 clockwork figures which move to the sound of music. The Archbishop's sense of humour was decidedly adolescent: he had fountains installed in unlikely places which were activated to drench his guests unexpectedly. The fountains are still in working order, and are demonstrated on tours of Schloss Hellbrunn, which is easily reached from Salzburg within minutes. It was at Hellbrunn that the first opera performances outside Italy were staged in 1618. The operas were Andromeda (probably by Giacobbi) and Monteverdi's *Orfeo*.

(The palace was designed by Santino Solari, so the theatre is presumably also by Solari.)

Hellbrunn, mechan. Theater

61

KARLSRUHE, *Germany* (*B.R.D.*)
HOFTHEATER

HE old theatre built by Weinbrenner and opened in 1808 was famous throughout Germany through Goethe's description of it as '*mustergültig*' (setting a standard). Plays and operas of Schiller, Goethe, Shakespeare and Mozart were its staple fare. During a performance in 1847, an open gas flame caught a drapery and the theatre burned to the ground. Sixty-three people lost their lives in the fire. The new house, depicted on the postcard, was designed by Heinrich Hübsch and opened on 17 May 1853 with Schiller's *Jungfrau von Orleans* and, a few days later, Gluck's *Armide*. The first complete stage performance of Berlioz's *Les Troyens* was given under Felix Mottl in 1890. The revolution of 1918 altered the theatre's status from that of Grossherzogliches Hoftheater (literally Grand Ducal Court Theatre) to that of Badisches Landestheater (Baden Provincial Theatre), and in 1933 it became the Badisches Staatstheater or State Theatre. It was destroyed by bombs in 1944: the ruins were not demolished and cleared away until 1963.

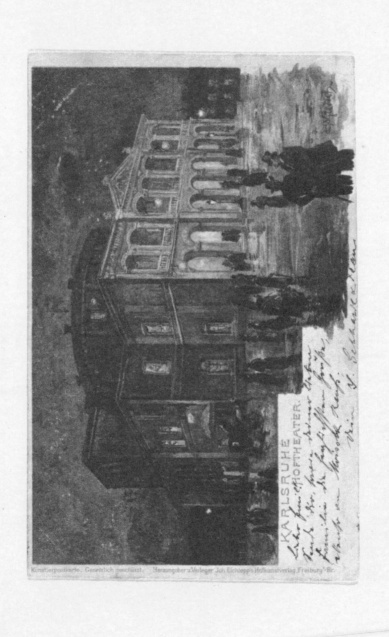

LEIPZIG, *Germany* (*D.D.R.*)

NEUES THEATER

THE Neues Theater (New Theatre) in what was then called the Augustusplatz was designed by the Berlin architect Carl Ferdinand Langhans. It took from 1864 to 1868 to build, and was much influenced by Von Knobelsdorff's Berlin Staatsoper and Schinkel's Berlin Schauspielhaus. It was opened in 1869 primarily as an opera house. Under the administration of Angelo Neumann, it became the base of the Wagner company which gave the first performances of the *Ring* in London, Amsterdam, Brussels, Venice and several other European cities. From 1878 to 1889 Artur Nikisch was chief conductor here, and from 1886 to 1888 his assistant was Gustav Mahler. Important premieres in the twen-

tieth century include those of Křenek's *Jonny spielt auf* (1927) and Kurt Weill's *Rise and Fall of the City of Mahagonny* (1930). It is the only theatre to have produced all of Wagner's operas, including the incomplete *Die Feen*, *Die Hochzeit*, *Das Liebesverbot* and *Die Feen*, which it performed in two cycles in chronological order in 1938. (Leipzig was Wagner's birthplace.) The theatre was destroyed by bombs in December 1943. For several years the opera company performed elsewhere, but between 1956 and 1960 a new opera house was built on the site of the Neues Theater, the square on which it stands having now changed its name to Karl Marx-Platz. The new Opera House opened in 1960.

LEIPZIG   Neues Theater

Herzliche Grüsse & Küsse
an Dich Emil & Ihr Kinder
von mir & Sepp. Es geht
🔔 Dr. Trenkler Co., Leipzig. 1903. 71g 74.

65

LIGNICE (Legnica), *Poland*

STADTTHEATER

At the time of the postcard, Lignice was the small Silesian town of Liegnitz, and part of the German Reich. Its theatre was built between 1839 and 1842 to designs by Carl Ferdinand Langhans, son of Carl Gotthard Langhans who designed several theatres as well as the Brandenburg Gate in Berlin. Carl Ferdinand worked under Schinkel in the 1830s and also designed theatres in Breslau (Wrocław), Stettin and Dessau. The theatre was still in use for opera and drama in the 1930s, when it had a seating capacity of some 600.

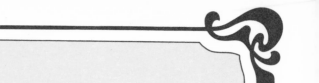

67

LJUBLJANA, *Yugoslavia*

THEATER

T HE town of Ljubljana was called Laibach in the days when Slovenia, of which it is the chief town, was an Austrian province. Its all-purpose theatre was called simply Theater, and is still called that, though now in another tongue: 'Gledališče'. The theatre, which is still in use for opera and ballet, opened on 29 September 1892 with a Slovakian historical drama, *Veronika Deseniška*. It replaced an earlier theatre on the same site which had existed from 1867 until destroyed by fire in 1887.

The new theatre, designed by local architects J. V. Hrásky and Ant. Hrúby, became the centre for Slovenian nationalism. The Slovenians shared the building with the German-speaking section of the community, but German performances were given less frequently because they were boycotted by a patriotic Slovenian public. In 1913 the German-speaking Austrians built their own theatre, designed by Alexander Graf. This is now the drama theatre of Ljubljana, while the 1892 theatre shown on the postcard houses the opera.

LJUBLJANA. — LAIBACH.
Gledišče. — Theater.

69

LVOV, *U.S.S.R.*
STÄDTISCHES THEATER

THE Soviet city of Lvov in the Ukraine is the Polish Lwow which was ceded by Poland in 1939. Before 1919, it was the capital of Galicia, a province of Austro-Hungary, and known by its German-language name, Lemberg. Its Civic Theatre or 'Teatr miejski' was built in the years 1897 to 1900. Known now as the Ivan Franko Academic Theatre for Opera and Ballet, it is still in use: a recent photograph shows it and its surroundings to have undergone no change at all since the turn of the century. There have been changes in Lemberg-Lvov, however, for this busy Soviet industrial city of well over half a million inhabitants had only 160,000 when the theatre was built, and a good quarter of them were Jewish. The 1903 Baedeker for Austro-Hungary reveals that, at that time, 'Polish plays and Polish-Italian operas are performed (the solos generally in Italian, the chorus in Polish).'

Nakł. M. R. Lwów.

Teatr miejski. Städtisches Theater.

71

MARIÁNSKÉ LÁZNĚ, *Czechoslovakia*

THEATER

ARIÁNSKÉ Lázně was, in Austro-Hungarian days, the famous watering place, Marienbad. It is still a popular spa in Czechoslovakia. The theatre, which is still in operation, was originally built by a local architect, Friedrich Zickler, between 1867–69. In the form in which it is shown on the postcard (its message on the verso is dated 18 July 1914), the theatre is seen as it was, and is now, after being rebuilt during the years 1895–1904 by Walcher, a Viennese architect.

Marienbad. Waldquellstraße   Theater

MUNICH, *Germany* (*B.R.D.*)
NATIONALTHEATER

HERE have been three Bavarian national opera houses on the same site in the Max Joseph Platz; the one depicted is the second. The first theatre, the Hof- und Nationaltheater, constructed to designs by Karl von Fischer, was opened in 1818 and destroyed by fire in 1823. Immediately rebuilt by Leo von Klenze and reopened on 2 January 1825, the theatre remained in use until destroyed by bombs in 1943. Famous throughout Europe, the company of the Bavarian Court Opera, later the National Opera, has included at one time or another almost every German singer of distinction, as well as several international non-German artists. Hans von Bülow was Music Director from 1867 to 1869,

Bruno Walter from 1911 to 1922, Hans Knappertsbusch from 1922 to 1934 and Clemens Krauss from 1937 until the theatre's destruction. Post-war Music Directors have included Georg Solti and Rudolf Kempe. There is a strong tradition of Wagner and Richard Strauss performance at the National-theater, many of Strauss's operas having been conducted there by the composer himself. *Tristan und Isolde* (1865) and *Die Meistersinger von Nürnberg* (1868) are among the Wagner operas which were first staged in the theatre. Strauss's final opera, *Capriccio*, was given its premiere there in 1942.

It was restored after the war, and reopened in 1963 with Strauss's *Die Frau ohne Schatten*.

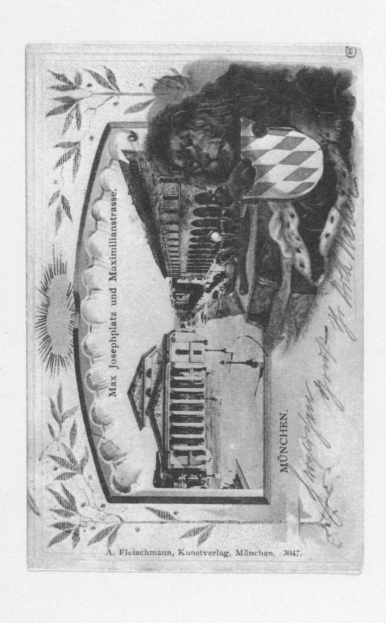

Max Josephplatz und Maximilianstrasse.

MÜNCHEN.

A. Fleischmann, Kunstverlag, München. 3047.

MUNICH, *Germany* (*B.R.D.*)
THEATER AM GÄRTNERPLATZ

THIS 932-seat theatre was built in 1864–65 by the architect Reiffenstuel Senior, and opened in the same year. It serves as the Volksoper, or vernacular opera and operetta house for Munich, producing the lighter operas and operettas with its own company which is only rarely augmented by the engagement of guest artists. The theatre was severely damaged during the war but was repaired soon afterwards and is now in use all the year round.

München. Gärtnerplatz und Theater

2624

77

MUNICH, *Germany* (*B.R.D.*)
PRINZ REGENTEN-THEATER

HIS side view of Munich's Prinz Regenten-Theater dates from the first decade of the century, when the theatre was new. Seating 1122, it was built in 1900 to designs by Heilmann and Littmann, and opened on 20 August 1901 with a performance of Act III of Wagner's *Die Meistersinger von Nürnberg*. The rest of the evening was no doubt taken up with speeches. Constructed on Bayreuth principles, the theatre was intended, from the beginning, as Munich's answer to Bayreuth: a theatre for the music dramas of Wagner. In due course, operas by composers other than Wagner were admitted into the repertoire. When the National Theatre, home of the Bavarian State Opera, was destroyed during the 1939–45 war, the Prinz Regenten-Theater became the company's home from 1945 until 1963 when the rebuilt Nationaltheater was opened. Since then, the Prinz Regenten-Theater has been in use only occasionally, and at present it is closed.

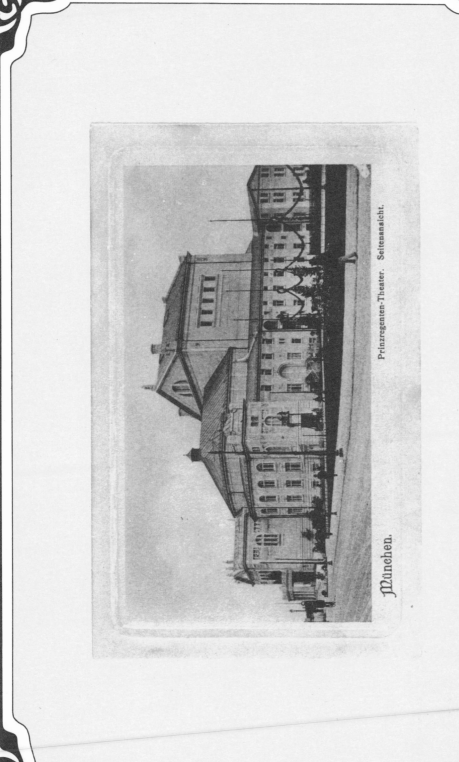

München. Prinzregenten-Theater. Seitenansicht.

NUREMBERG, *Germany* (*B.R.D.*)
NEUES STADTTHEATER

THE Civic Theatre and Opera House was built in 1904–05 to designs by Heinrich Seeling, and opened on 1 September 1905. Its stagehouse was completely rebuilt in 1935 by Professor Paul Schultze-Naumburg. Damaged during the Second World War, it was restored in 1945 and is still in use as an opera house, and called Opernhaus to distinguish from the city's other Civic theatres.

Nürnberg, Neues Stadttheater.

ORADEA, *Romania*
SZIGETI SZÍNHÁZ

ORADEA, now in Romania, on the western edge of Transylvania, is one of the most ancient Hungarian towns, Nagyvárad. In Austro-Hungarian times, it was also known by the German name of Grosswardein. The theatre was built in 1899–1900 by the Viennese architects Fellner and Helmer, and opened on 15 October 1900 with a mixed programme of Hungarian plays, operetta excerpts and poetry. It seats 1000, and its building was made possible by donations from the business community of Grosswardein. The theatre, which is still in use for opera and drama, is in the centre of the town and is now known as Teatrul de Stat.

NAGYVÁRAD. Szigeti szinház

PLAUEN, *Germany (D.D.R.)*

STADT THEATER

HE Civic Theatre of the small industrial town of Plauen, in Saxony, was built by Baurat Arwed Rossbach in 1898 and opened in the autumn of that year. The first opera to be performed there was Weber's *Der Freischütz* in October 1899. The theatre was damaged during the Second World War, but restoration was begun early in 1945. Most of the interior dates from this restoration, though the greater part of the façade is in its original state. As early as October 1945 the theatre was reopened with a performance of Mozart's *Le nozze di Figaro.*

Stadt-Theather

Gruss aus Plauen i. V. 23. 9. 1905.

PLZEŇ, *Czechoslovakia*
STADTTHEATER

ORMERLY Pilsen, and still noted for its beer, the Bohemian town of Plzeň supports two theatres. This, the larger of the two, was constructed between 1898 and 1902 to designs by Antonín Balšánek, and seats 1001. It is still in use. A joint resident company of the two theatres presents opera, operetta, ballet and drama.

POTSDAM, *Germany (D.D.R.)*
SCHAUSPIELHAUS

HE theatre was built in 1793–98 by Georg Friedrich Boumann, a Potsdam architect and artillery officer, after original designs by Carl Gotthard Langhans. (Boumann also executed another Langhans theatre, that in Schloss Charlottenburg, Berlin, in 1788–89.) Used exclusively for drama, the theatre was probably destroyed in the 1939–45 war. It is not to be confused with the still extant little theatre in the Neues Palais at Potsdam, built in the years 1763–69 for Frederick the Great. Potsdam, the capital of Brandenburg, is 18 miles south-east of Berlin.

Potsdam, 17.05.

B&B 512 L. Saalfeld, Berlin SW. 29

Schauspielhaus

Herzl. Gruß! Wm. Holz.

Stadttheater

POZNÁN, *Poland*
TEATR POLSKI

HE theatre was opened on 21 June 1875, having been built with funds donated by the Polish people who, at that time, were forbidden to produce plays in Polish at the larger Stadttheater. During the period of the Prussian partition, the Teatr Polski or Polish Theatre became the centre of Polish nationalism, and until the 1890s was the only theatre in German Poland where productions were given in Polish.

In 1918, the town, which was still known by its German name, Posen, became the Polish town of Poznán, and its two theatres were combined under the title Teatry Miejskie (Civic Theatres). Since 1923, the former Stadttheater, now the Wielki, has staged opera and ballet, leaving drama to the Polski which was nationalized in 1946. In 1965, *Le Théâtre en Pologne* said: 'This stage has rendered outstanding social and artistic services, has given many excellent presentations and is associated with the names of famous artists.'

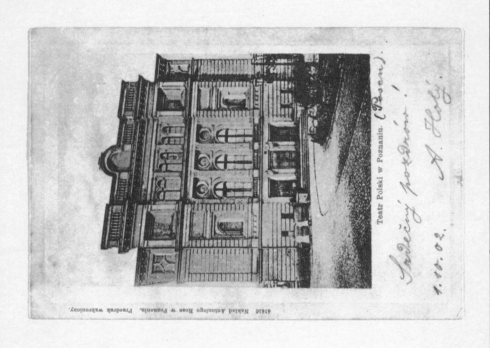

Teatr Polski w Poznaniu. (Posen).

41416 Nakład Antoniego Rose w Poznaniu. Przedruk wzbroniony.

Serdeczny pozdrów!
1.10.02.   A. Flaz

POZNÁN, *Poland*
STADTTHEATER

AN earlier Stadttheater closed in 1874, and the building depicted on the card opened in 1879 as the principal German theatre of the town, then called Posen. Performances of opera, ballet and drama were given. In 1909–10 the theatre was rebuilt by the famous Munich theatre architects Heilmann and Littmann.

In 1918, Posen became Polish and the Stadttheater's name was changed to Teatr Wielki or Great Theatre. It and the Teatr Polski became Poznán's two civic theatres. Since 1923, the Teatr Wielki has specialized in opera and ballet, and in the years between the two world wars it housed what was considered the finest opera company in Poland. In 1949 the theatre was nationalized: it still has a fine reputation in Poland for opera.

Posen. Wilhelmsplatz m. Stadttheater.

m. d. l. Gr.! A. Holz.

5. X. 01.

LOUIS GLASER LEIPZIG. 9106

PRAGUE, *Czechoslovakia*
NÁRODNI DIVADLO

ZECHOSLOVAKIA's Národni Divadlo, or National Theatre, came into being as the result of a movement which began in 1850 and which, in 1862, produced a Provisional Theatre, directed for some years by the composer Smetana. The building of the permanent theatre began in 1868, to designs by Josef Zítek, and the theatre opened in 1881 with the premiere of Smetana's *Libuše*, only to be destroyed by fire two months later. Within four weeks sufficient funds had been collected by donation to rebuild, and the new theatre was opened in 1883 again with *Libuše*. The reconstruction was supervized by the architect Josef Schulz who improved on Zítek's original designs. The technical equipment and decorations were also superior to those of the first building. The theatre now seats 1598.

Many important Czech operas of the nineteenth and twentieth centuries have had their premieres at the National Theatre, among them Dvořák's *Rusalka* (1901), Janáček's *Mr Brouček's Excursion to the Moon* (1920) and Martinu's *Juliette* (1938). The theatre is shared by the national opera and theatre companies.

Gruss aus Prag!

Blick von der neuen Brücke auf das Nationaltheater. — 87.

Carl Bellmann in Prag. 902. 292.

PRAGUE, *Czechoslovakia*
NEUES DEUTSCHES THEATER

PRAGUE's New German Theatre is today called the Smetanovo Divadlo or Smetana Theatre. It was built in the years 1885 to 1887 by the German community of Prague as a protest against the construction of the Czech National Theatre, and opened on 5 January 1888 with Wagner's *Die Meistersinger von Nürnberg*. Its architects were Fellner and Helmer, and the sculptural decoration on the roof, representing the chariot of Dionysos and Thalia, is by Theodor Friedl. It seats 1554. For many years the theatre was considered one of the most important German-language opera houses outside Germany. The young Gustav Mahler who had been engaged as conductor in 1885 by the German Opera, and had given notable performances of Wagner's *Ring*, also conducted in the new theatre. On Mahler's recommendation, Otto Klemperer was engaged between 1907 and 1910. One of the last German-language premieres before the Second World War was that of Křenek's *Karl V*. With its name changed in 1948 to Smetana Theatre, it became the second house of the National Opera.

Gruss aus Prag!

Das neue deutsche Theater. — 86.

95

ROSTOCK, *Germany* (*D.D.R.*)
THEATER

Built in 1894–95 by Heinrich Seeling, this civic theatre staged opera, operetta and drama. It was completely destroyed in 1942.

Heinrich Seeling was one of the most successful of German theatre architects. His buildings include the Stadttheaters in Halle, Essen, Bromberg (now Bydgoszcz), Kiel and Kreiburg; the rebuilding of Aachen in 1901, the rebuilding of Braunschweig in 1904, and the Deutsches Opernhaus, Berlin, in 1911–12.

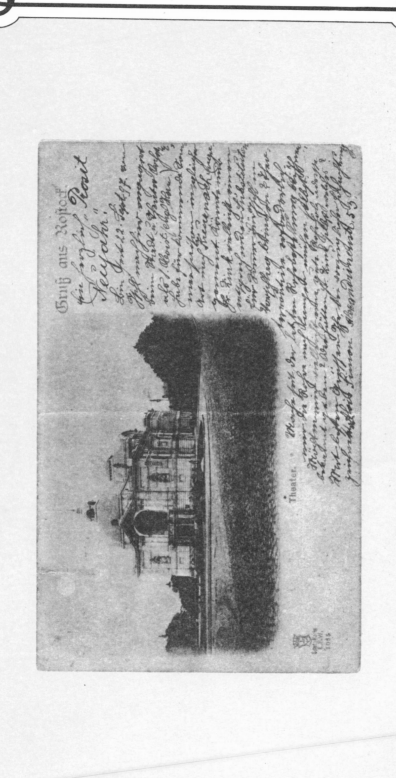

97

SCHWERIN, *Germany* (*D.D.R.*)
HOFTHEATER

THE Hoftheater, which subsequently became the Landestheater and is now called the Mecklenburgisches Staatstheater, was built in 1882–86 to designs by Georg Daniel, a Mecklenburg architect, and opened on 3 October 1886. As the Court Theatre of Mecklenburg, it presented a mixed programme of opera, operetta and plays. The theatre still exists.

STRASBOURG, *France*

THEATER

STRASBOURG was captured during the Franco-German war of 1870, and was a German town at the time of the postcard; hence the spelling 'Strasburg'. It was regained by France in 1918. The Stadttheater, now the Théâtre Municipal, was built in the years 1817–21 to designs by the city architect, Jean Villot. During the siege of 1870, it was burnt out, and was restored to its original condition between 1872–75 by the new German administration. The stage house was heightened to take the counterweight system which had not been invented at the time of the initial installation. In 1888 additional accommodation, including new dressing rooms, a library and costume stores, was added by Stadtbaumeister Ott. Many operas have been given their French premières in the theatre, which is still in use.

STRASSBURG i. E.   Theater

Mit meine beste Grüße!
J. Hubbay

STUTTGART, *Germany* (*B.R.D.*)
KÖNIGLICHES HOFTHEATER

STUTTGART'S Königliches Hoftheater (Royal Court Theatre) was first converted from a *Lusthaus*, or summer palace, by Leopold Retti in 1750. It was rebuilt by Pierre Louis-Philippe de la Guépière in 1758, and subsequently underwent further alterations and rebuildings. Used mostly for opera and ballet, the Hoftheater was on the north side of the Schloss Platz, between the Königin Olga-Bau (Queen Olga Building) and the Residenz-Schloss. It burned down on the night of 19–20 January 1902, less than a year after the postcard depicting it was sent. (The present opera house was opened in 1912, during which year Richard Strauss's *Ariadne auf Naxos*, in its first version, had its premiere there, conducted by the composer.)

Kgl. Hoftheater u. Königin Olga-Bau

STUTTGART 3/4 1901.

No. 301. Verlag von G. Haußler, Stuttgart.

STUTTGART, *Germany (B.R.D.)*

WILHELMA THEATER

THE Royal Wilhelma Theatre, built in 1838–40, designed by Carl Zanth, was in the Cannstadt district of Stuttgart, in the park just north of the Schloss Garten which connects it with the main Residenz-Schloss. Much smaller than the Königliches Hoftheater in the centre of the town, it was, at the time of the postcard, Stuttgart's second theatre and was the scene of much operatic and theatrical activity, as well as concerts.

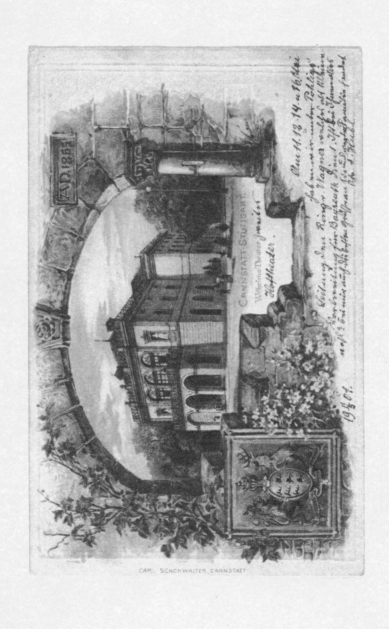

STUTTGART, *Germany* (*B.R.D.*)
INTERIMTHEATER

ALSO known as the Neues Hoftheater, the Interimtheater or 'temporary theatre' was erected in 1902, immediately after the destruction by fire of the old Königliches Hoftheater. The Hoftheater had burned down in January; plans were begun for the theatre in April, and it opened later the same year, on 12 October, its building having cost 680,000 Marks. The architects were Eisenlohr and Weigle.

(In due course, the Interimtheater was replaced by Max Littmann's splendid new theatre which was begun in 1909 and opened in 1912. Its architect claimed it was the first double auditorium theatre which completely solved the old problem of multi-purpose use. It is a splendid vindication of the system of Royal patronage—in this case by King Wilhelm II of Württemberg—operating in the fragmented states of pre-1918 Germany.)

The postcard on which the Interimtheater is depicted is postmarked 30 December 1902, two months after its opening.

Stuttgart. Königl. Hoftheater (Interimtheater). 30.12.02.

Verlag von G. Haußer, Stuttgart.

SZCZECIN, *Poland*
STADTTHEATER

A T the time of the postcard, Szczecin was part of the German Reich and was called Stettin. It was the capital of Pomerania and was regarded as the port of Berlin. The town was severely bombed during the Second World War and the theatre was destroyed. It was a typical all-purpose theatre, housing drama as well as opera, and was built by Carl Ferdinand Langhans from 1846–49, opening with Goethe's *Egmont* on 21 October 1849. The wing projecting forward from the semi-circle of the auditorium block was added in 1899. It contained new foyers and staircases.

Stettin. — Das Stadttheater.

TEPLICE, *Czechoslovakia*
THEATER

THE small watering place and industrial town of Teplice, north-west of Prague, was known as Teplitz when Czechoslovakia was part of Austro-Hungary. The theatre in its Schönau district was built by Turba and Zitek in collaboration with the architect Martin Schreiber from Dresden. Constructed between 1872 and 1874, it was opened in the latter year. The theatre no longer exists, having been destroyed by fire in 1919.

TEPLITZ – SCHÖNAU.

Theater.

111

VIENNA, *Austria*
CARL THEATER

THE Carl Theater, demolished in 1951, stood in Vienna's Praterstrasse, on the site of the old Leopoldstädter Theater which existed from 1781 to 1847 when it was demolished and replaced by the Carl Theater. The Leopoldstädter Theater had been famous for its productions of the *Zauberpossen* or magic plays of Nestroy and Raimund. The Carl Theater, named after its impresario, Karl Carl, was constructed to designs by Eduard van der Nüll and August Siccardsburg, the architects who twenty years later were to build the Vienna Opera House. It took only seven months to build, and opened in December 1847. Between 1854 and 1860 Nestroy himself ran the theatre. Franz von Suppé's first

operetta, *Das Pensionat*, was produced there in 1860. In 1895 alterations were made to the auditorium by Wegmann, which entailed the removal of the fourth gallery. The theatre now seated 1121. It closed its doors in 1929, was severely damaged during air raids in 1944, and was finally cleared away in 1951.

Among the many famous operettas first produced at the Carl Theater are Franz von Suppé's *Boccacio* (1879), Johann Strauss's *Wiener Blut* (1899: four months after Strauss's death), Leo Fall's *Die Dollar Prinzessin* (1907), Oscar Straus's *Ein Walzertraum* (1907) and Franz Lehár's *Zigeunerliebe* (1910).

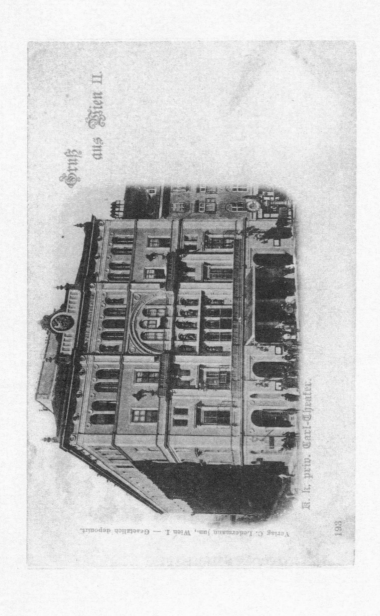

Gruß aus Wien II

K. k. priv. Carl-Theater.

Verlag C. Ledermann jun., Wien I. — Gesetzlich deponirt.

193

VIENNA, *Austria*
KAISERJUBILÄUMSSTADTTHEATER

THE theatre was built within ten months in 1898, to designs by Franz von Krauss and Alexander Graf, and opened in December of that year with Kleist's *Hermannsschlacht*. It seated 1850. Named to celebrate fifty years of the Emperor Franz Josef's reign, the theatre soon became known as the Volksoper, since its repertoire largely consisted of the lighter operas and operettas. When the Staatsoper was destroyed by bombs in 1945, the company moved to the Volksoper at the end of the war, and re-opened the theatre with Mozart's *Le nozze de Figaro* conducted by Josef Krips. For the following ten years the company of the Staatsoper played in the Volksoper and the old Theater an der Wien. In 1955, when the rebuilt Staatsoper opened its doors, the Volksoper reverted to its policy of operetta and popular opera in the vernacular. Between 1961 and 1963, the theatre was enlarged and renovated, and in 1973 the auditorium was redecorated and given new seating. Today the Volksoper flourishes as Vienna's second opera house and the home also of Viennese operetta of the nineteenth and early twentieth centuries, the so-called Gold and Silver eras of operetta.

Gruß aus Wien IX.

Kaiser-Jubiläums-Stadttheater.

C. Ledermann jr. Wien I.

1757

115

VIENNA, *Austria*
K.U.K. HOFOPER

HE Imperial and Royal Court Opera became, after the fall of the Habsburgs and the end of the Austro-Hungarian Empire, the Vienna Staatsoper. Designed by Eduard van der Nüll and August Siccard von Siccardsburg in 1860–61, the opera house on the Ring was opened in 1869 with a performance of Mozart's *Don Giovanni*. The problems encountered during the construction of the building, and the carping of the Viennese, drove Van der Nüll to suicide before the opening. Von Siccardsburg had a stroke and died, heartbroken, a few months later.

Under Gustav Mahler (1897–1907), the company reached its greatest heights: the enormous reputation which the Vienna Opera still enjoys can be traced directly back to the Mahler period. It continued until the beginning of the 1939–45 war to have the best opera ensemble in Europe, with such singers as Lotte Lehmann, Maria Jeritza, Elisabeth

Schumann, Richard Tauber, Alfred Piccaver, Vera Schwarz and conductors of the calibre of Bruno Walter, Josef Krips and Clemens Krauss.

Its stage and auditorium almost completely gutted by bombs in 1945, the Staatsoper was rebuilt, and opened again in 1955 with Beethoven's *Fidelio* conducted by Karl Böhm. In the fifties and sixties, it again boasted a superb company of prewar singers such as Dermota, Kunz, Hilde Konetzni, Paul Schoeffler and Julius Patzak, as well as such younger artists as Elisabeth Schwarzkopf, Irmgard Seefried, Hilde Gueden, Lisa della Casa, Leonie Rysanek, Christa Ludwig, Sena Jurinac, Wilma Lipp and Ljuba Welitsch. Although the stage and auditorium of the Staatsoper date from 1955, the exterior walls, the original foyer and staircase still remain, and Rodin's bust of Mahler is to be found in the upstairs foyer.

Wien

K. k. Hofoper

117

VIENNA, *Austria*

JOHANN STRAUSS THEATER

HE theatre, which stood in the Favoritenstrasse, was built in 1908 to plans by Eduard Prandl, and opened in October of that year with Strauss's *1001 Nights*. It seated 1192. It was completely re-modelled in 1931, was renamed the Scala and be-came a cinema. After the end of the Second World War, it served the Russian occupying forces as a theatre again until 1956. After much discussion concerning its future, the theatre was finally demo-lished in 1959–60.

Wien, IV.
Johann Strauß-Theater.

119

Built in 1893, to plans by Franz Roth, and seating 1413, the Raimund Theater opened in that year with a performance of *Die gefesselte Phantaisie* by Ferdinand Raimund, the playwright after whom it was named. A bust of Raimund stands in the portico. A non-municipal, privately owned theatre, it has always specialized in the production of operettas, which are performed by its resident company. One of the most popular Viennese operettas to have its premiere at the Raimund Theater was *Das Dreimäderlhaus*, known in English as *Lilac Time*, whose score by Heinrich Berté was adapted from the music of Schubert. *Das Dreimäderlhaus* was given its first performance at the Raimund Theater in 1916, and has occasionally been revived there. Robert Stolz's *Der Tanz ins Glück* was given its premiere in 1920. The theatre retains its reputation for authentic productions of the older Viennese operettas of Johann Strauss, Emmerich Kálmán, Leo Fall, Oscar Straus and others, including of course Franz Lehár.

Raimund-Theater.

Gruß aus Wien VI.

Verlag C. Ledermann jun., Wien I. — Gesetzlich deponirt.

320

WARSAW, *Poland*
TEATR WIELKI

HE foundation stone of the Teatr Wielki, or Great Theatre, was laid on 19 November 1825, and the theatre, designed by Antonio Corazzi who was responsible for several other important buildings in Warsaw, was opened in February 1833 with a performance of Rossini's *Il barbiere di Siviglia*. The enormous building in fact housed not only the Teatr Wielki which was used mainly for opera and large-scale theatrical productions, but also the Narodowy (the National Theatre for drama) and the Nowy (formerly the Sale Redutowe). The entire building was burnt out during the siege of Warsaw in 1939 and suffered further damage in the uprising of five years later.

The right wing was rebuilt in 1949 as the National Theatre, and by 1965 the entire building had been restored by Bohdan Pniewski. Now, in addition to theatres for opera and drama, it houses a ballet school, an opera studio, and Poland's Theatre Museum.

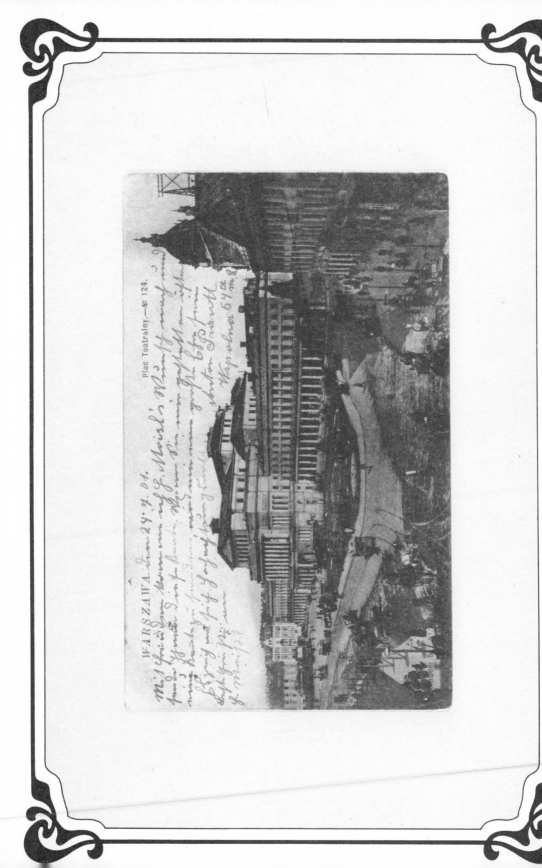

WEIMAR, *Germany* (*D.D.R.*)
THEATER

FOUR theatres have occupied the same site in the old Thuringian town of Weimar, of which the one on the postcard is the third. (The first Weimar Hoftheater was opened in 1780, altered in 1791, and rebuilt in 1798 by Thouret. Goethe became director of this theatre in 1791, a post he held for twenty-two years. The theatre was burned down in 1825.) This theatre was built in six months, opening in September 1825. It enjoyed a distinguished reputation for many years, especially between 1847 and 1858 when Liszt was in charge, and Von Bülow one of the conductors. Among the important works which had their premieres here are Wagner's *Lohengrin* (1850), Schubert's *Alfonso und Estrella* (1854), Cornelius's *Der Barbier von Bagdad* (1858), Humperdinck's *Hänsel und Gretel* (1893) and Richard Strauss's *Guntram* while Strauss was chief conductor at Weimar in 1894. By 1906 the theatre was thought to have become inadequate; it was demolished and replaced by a fourth theatre in 1906–08, designed by Heilmann and Littmann, which flourished until damaged by bombs in 1945. Again it was rebuilt, and reopened in 1948. In 1973 it was closed for extensive reconstruction, and has been in use once more since 1975. It is now known as the Deutsches Nationaltheater. The present building is basically that of Heilmann and Littmann, though the interior is new.

ZAGREB, *Yugoslavia*
KROATISCHES LANDESTHEATER

THE Croatian Provincial Theatre in Zagreb, the town formerly known by its German name, Agram, was constructed in 1895, to designs by Fellner and Helmer. It opened with a performance of the first Croatian national opera, *Nikola Šubić Zrinski* by Ivan Zajc. The theatre was closed between 1902 and 1909, but since then has maintained regular performances, except during the war years. Several singers from the Zagreb opera have made successful international careers, among them Sena Jurinac and Zinka Milanov. Known today simply as Kazalište or theatre, the building houses both opera and drama.

Zagreb — Agram Hrv. zem. kazalište. — Kroatisches Landestheater

ACKNOWLEDGMENTS

Among those who have very kindly helped me with information are my friends Mr. Jiří Mucha of Prague; Dr. Horst Seeger, Intendant of the Dresden Opera; Dr. Brigitte Lohmeyer of the German Embassy in London; Frau Lolly Müller of the Österreichischer Bundestheaterverband, Vienna; Dr. Ranka Kuic of Belgrade University; and Miss Eva Metzler of London. I am grateful also to the Austrian Institute, the German Institute, the Cultural Counsellor at the Swiss Embassy and the London Correspondent of the Novosti Press Agency.

My special thanks are due to Mr. Victor Glasstone, who provided me with architectural information concerning several theatres, who read my manuscript and gave me much helpful advice.

Designed by Paul Turner